Sing Along - Sign Along
with
Spanish

All music and lyrics by:

...bringing Spanish to life!

Time to Sign, Inc. | PO Box 33831, Indialantic FL 32940 | P 321.726.9466 | F321.726.9467

Table of Contents

Boca Beth Theme Song
La Canción thema de Boca Beth

Yo quiero hablar Español.
I want to speak Spanish.

¡Yo quiero hacerlo ahora!
I want to do it NOW!

Y o   q u i e r o   h a b l a r   I n g l é s .
I   w a n t   t o   s p e a k   E n g l i s h .

¡ Y o   q u i e r o   h a c e r l o   a h o r a !
I   w a n t   t o   d o   i t   N O W !

(repeat one more time)

What's Your Name?

¿Cómo te llamas?

¿Cómo   Te   Llamas?
What's   Your   Name? Repeat twice

¿Cómo   Te   Llamas   Amigo?

Me   llamo   Tommy.
My   name is   Tommy. Repeat twice

Me   llamo   Tommy.

What's   Your   Name?
¿Cómo   Te   Llamas?   Repeat twice

What's   your   name   friend?

My   name is   Rosa
Me   llamo   Rosa. Repeat twice

My   name is   Rosa.

¿Cómo   Te   Llamas?
What's   Your   Name? Repeat twice

¿Cómo   Te   Llamas   Amigo?

Me   llamo   BOCA.
My   name is   BOCA. Repeat twice

Me   llamo   BOCA.

Here & There?

¿Aquí y Allí?

Aquí,
Here,

Aquí
Here!

Allí,
There,

Allí
There!

Aquí,
Here,

Aquí
Here!

Copyright © 2009 Time to Sign, Inc.

Allí,
There,

Allí
There!

Aquí means here,   Allí means there.

Aquí then Allí means here then there!

Getting Ready
Preparando

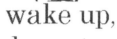

I   wake up,   I wake up   every day.
Me   levanto, levanto   cada día.

   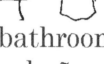

I use the bathroom, the bathroom every day.
Uso   el   baño,   el baño   cada día.

I wash my hands, wash my hands every day.
Me lavo mis manos,   mis manos   cada día.

I   comb my hair,   comb my hair   every day.
Me   peino mi pelo,   mi pelo   cada día.

I   get   dressed,   get   dressed   every day.
Me pongo mi ropa,   mi ropa   cada día.

I eat my breakfast,   my breakfast every day.
Tomo desayuno,   desayuno   cada día.

I brush my teeth, my teeth every day.
Cepillo mis dientes, dientes cada día.

I start the day with a smile every day.
Comienzo con una sonrisa, sonrisa cada día.

I share my joy, my joy every day.
Comparto mi felicidad, felicidad cada día.

I can do it , do it every day.
Puedo hacerlo, hacerlo cada día.

Five Little Monkeys
Cinco monitos

Five   little   monkeys   jumping on the bed!

One fell off and bumped his head!

Mommy called the doctor and the doctor said,

No   more   monkeys   jumpin' on the bed!

Copyright © 2008 Time to Sign, Inc.

¡Cuatro   monitos   saltando en la cama!

¡Uno se cayó   y golpeó la cabeza!

¡Mama llamó al doctor y el doctor dijo!

¡Que no más monos saltan en la cama!

Three little monkeys jumping on the bed!

One fell off and bumped his head!

Mommy called the doctor and the doctor said,

No more monkeys jumpin' on the bed!

¡Dos   monitos   saltando en la cama!

¡Uno se cayó   y golpeó la cabeza!

¡Mama llamó al doctor y el doctor dijo!

¡Que no más   monos saltan en la cama!

One   little   monkeys   jumping on the bed!

One fell off and bumped his head!

Mommy called the doctor and the doctor said,

No   more   monkeys   jumpin' on the bed!

Let's Spell Animals
Deletriemos Animales

Let's   spell   c-a-t,   c-a-t,   c-a-t,
(We'll)

Let's   spell   c-a-t.   That   spells   cat.

Deletriemos   c-a-t,   c-a-t,   c-a-t,

Deletriemos   c-a-t,   Así   deletreas   cat.

Copyright © 2009 Time to Sign, Inc.

Let's   spell   d-o-g,   d-o-g,   d-o-g,
(We'll)

Let's   spell   d-o-g.   That   spells   dog.

Deletriemos   d-o-g,   d-o-g,   d-o-g,

Deletriemos   d-o-g,   Así   deletreas   dog.

Let's   spell   p-i-g,   p-i-g,   p-i-g,
(We'll)

Let's   spell   p-i-g.   That   spells   pig.

Deletriemos   p-i-g,   p-i-g,   p-i-g,

Deletriemos   p-i-g,   Así   deletreas   pig.

Position Song
Canción de posición

Top, top is encima, Encima is top.

Bottom is fondo. Fondo is bottom.

Over, over is sobre. Sobre is over.

Under is debajo. Debajo is under.

Left is izquierda. Izquierda is left.

Right is derecho. Derecho is right.

Inside is adentro. Adentro is inside.

Outside is afuera. Afuera is outside.

Senses
Sentidos

We	have	senses	that	we	use.
Tenemos	sentidos		que	usamos. (Repeat)	

I	see	with	my	eyes.
Yo	veo	con	mis	ojos. (Repeat)

I	hear	with	my	ears.
Yo	oigo	con	mis	orejas. (Repeat)

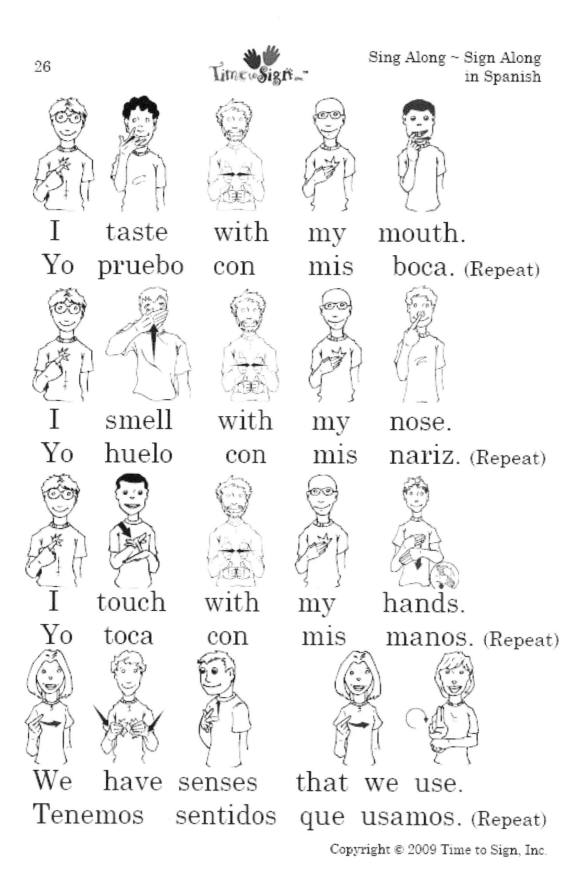

I taste with my mouth.
Yo pruebo con mis boca. (Repeat)

I smell with my nose.
Yo huelo con mis nariz. (Repeat)

I touch with my hands.
Yo toca con mis manos. (Repeat)

We have senses that we use.
Tenemos sentidos que usamos. (Repeat)

Adding Numbers

Sumar números

Adding   numbers is so much fun.

I   can   do it - you will see.

Sumar   números es divertido.

Puedo   hacerlos - ya verás.

One   plus   one   equals   two.

Add   along   with   me.

Uno   y   uno   son   dos,

suma   conmigo.   Me   gusta   sumar.

Adding   numbers is so much fun.

I   can   do it - you will see.

Sumar   números es divertido.

Puedo   hacerlos - ya verás.

Two   plus   Two   equals   four.

Add   along with   me.

Dos   y   dos   son   cuatro,

suma   conmigo.   I   like to   add.

Adding   numbers is so much fun.

I   can   do   it -   you   will   see.

Sumar   números es divertido.

Puedo   hacerlos -   ya   verás.

Five   plus   five   equals   ten.

Add   along   with   me.

Cinco   y   cinco   son   diez,

suma   conmigo.   Me   gusta   sumar.

More Shapes
Más formas

Diamond　　is　　diamante. (repeat 2 times)

I　　know　　my　　shapes.

Diamante　is　　diamond. (repeat 2 times)

Yo　　sé　　mis　　formas.

Star   is   estrella. (repeat 2 times)

I   know   my   shapes.

Estrella   is   star. (repeat 2 times)

Yo   sé   mis   formas.

Heart   is   corazón .   (repeat 2 times)

I   know   my   shapes.

Corazón   is   heart.   (repeat 2 times)

Yo   sé   mis   formas.

I See Animals
Veo Animales

I   see   a   tiger.
Veo   un   tigre.

He   has   stripes.
El   tiene   rayas.

He   likes   to run   fast.
El   le gusta   correr muy rapido.

I   see   an   elephant.
Veo   un   elefante.

He's so big.
El   es tan grande.

He   has a trunk   that is very long.
El   tiene una trompa que es muy larga.

I   see   a   lion.
Veo   un   león.

He's   is   a   king.
El   es un   rey.

The lion   roars   just like this.
El león   ruge   justo como asi.

Time to Sign

I   see   a   monkey.
Veo   un   mono.

He's   eats   bananas.
El   come   platanos.

The monkey makes a silly, silly noise.
El mono   hace un ruido tonto.

Time to Sign

Moovin' & Groovin'

Mueve y baila

Movin'   and   groovin'!

I like to move! I like to groove!

Mueve   y   baila!

Move and groove with me!

Follow the directions for the rest of the song.

The Weather Song
Canción de tiempo

It's   a   sunny   day.
Es   un   día   soleado.

I   see   the sun.
Veo   el sol.

The   sun   is   yellow.
El   sol   es   amarillo.

The   sun   is   bright.
El sol   es   brillante.

It's a   cloudy   day.
Es   un   día   nublado.

There are many   clouds.
Hay   muchas   nubes.

Time to Sign inc.™

Look   at the   clouds.
Mira   las   nubes.

The clouds   make it   shady.
Las nubes   dan   sombra.

It's a   rainy   day.
Es un   día   lluvioso.

I   see   the rain.
Veo la   lluvia.

We   feel   the rain.
Sentimos   la lluvia.

It   feels   good.
Se   siente   bien.

It's a   windy   day.
Es un   día   ventoso.

The wind   blows   fast.
El viento   sopla   rápido.

Look   at   the   leaves.
Mira   las   hojas.

I   like   the wind.
Me gusta   el viento.

More Opposites
Más opuestos

Sing opposites in Spanish & English.
Canta   en   Español y Inglés.

Sing   with   me! It's easy you'll   see!
¡Canta conmigo,   es   fácil   verás!

Largo   es   long,   long   is   largo.

Copyright © 2009 Time to Sign, Inc.

Corto es short, short is corto.

Largo - Corto! Long - Short!

Sing opposites in Spanish & English.
Canta en Español y Inglés.

Sing with me! It's easy you'll see!
¡Canta conmigo, es fácil verás!

Caliente es hot, hot is caliénte.

Frio es cold, cold is frio.

Caliente - Frio! Hot - Cold!

Sing opposites in Spanish & English.
Canta en Español y Inglés.

Sing with me! It's easy you'll see!
¡Canta conmigo, es fácil verás!

Lento es slow, slow is lento.

Rápido es fast, fast is rápido.

Lento - Rápido! Slow - Fast!

Sing opposites in Spanish & English.
Canta   en   Español y Inglés.

Sing   with   me!   It's easy   you'll   see!
¡Canta conmigo,   es   fácil   verás!

Abierto   es   open,   open   is   abierto.

Cerrado   es   closed,   closed   is   cerrado.

Abierto - Cerrado!   Open - Closed!

Singing   opposites!

What's Happenin'?
¿Qué pasa?

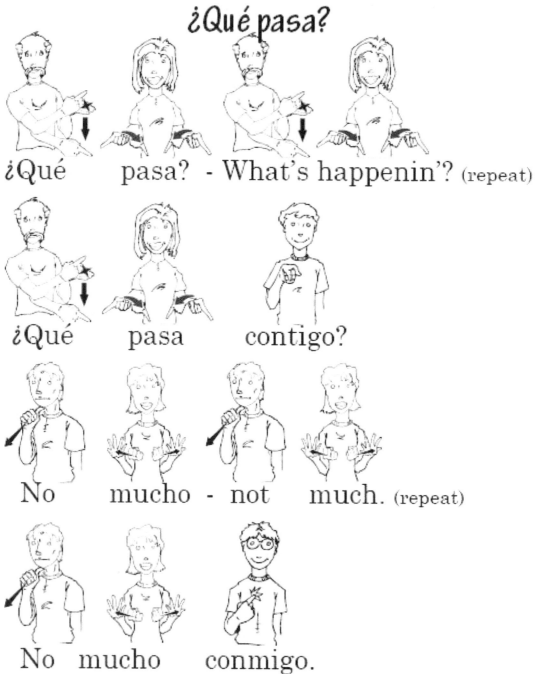

¿Qué   pasa? - What's happenin'? (repeat)

¿Qué   pasa   contigo?

No   mucho - not   much. (repeat)

No   mucho   conmigo.

Time to Sign™

What's happenin'? - ¿Qué pasa? (repeat)

What's happening with you?

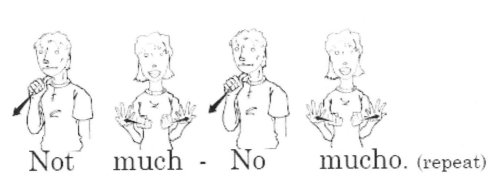

Not much - No mucho. (repeat)

Not much with me.

We Love You
Te Amamos

Mommy loves you, mommy loves you.

Yes I do, Yes I do.

Mommy loves you, mommy loves you.

Yes I do, Yes I do.

Daddy   loves   you,   daddy   loves   you.

Yes   I   do,   Yes   I   do.

Daddy   loves   you,   daddy   loves   you.

Yes   I   do,   Yes   I   do.

BOCA loves you, BOCA loves you.

Yes I do, Yes I do.

BOCA loves ____, BOCA loves ____.

Yes I do, Yes I do.

BOCA te ama,   BOCA   te   ama.

Sí lo hago,   sí   lo   hago

BOCA te _____, BOCA   te   _____.

Sí lo hago,   sí   lo   hago

Sign Language Handout
Opposites ~ Opuestos

Opposites
Opuestos

Long - Short
Largo - Corto

Hot - Cold
Caliente - Frio

Slow - Fast
Lento - Rápido

Open - Closed
Abierto - Cerrado

Top - Bottom
Encima - Fondo

Over - Under
Sobre - Debajo

Sign Language Handout
Senses ~ Sentidos

Senses
Sentidos

See
Veo

Hear
Oigo

Taste
Huelo

Smell
Pruebo

Touch
Toca

Sign Language Handout
Math/Numbers ~ Matemáticas/Números

Numbers
Números

Subrtact
Restar

Math
Matemáticas

Equals
Igual

Add
Sumar

 uno - one - 1   dos - two - 2

 tres - three - 3   cuatro - four - 4

 cinco - five - 5   seis - six - 6

 siete - seven - 7   ocho - eight - 8

 nueve - nine - 9   diez - ten - 10

Sign Language Handout
Shapes ~ Formas

Diamond
Diamante

Shapes
Formas

Heart
Corazón

Star
Estrella

Circle
Círculo

Square
Cuadrado

Oval
Ovalado

Sign Language Handout
Animals ~ Animales

Lion
León

Elephant
Elefante

Monkey
Mono

Tiger
Tigre

Dog
Perro

Cat
Gato

Pig
Cerdo

Animals
Animales

Copyright © 2009 Time to Sign, Inc.

Sign Language Handout
Weather ~ Clima

Clouds
Nubes

Weather
Clima

Snow
Nieve

Wind
Viento

Sun
Sol

Rain
lluvia

Book includes: Boca Beth Sing Along with Spanish Music CD.
Contact Time to Sign to be mailed CD directly.
Contact Time to Sign, Inc. to Order
www.TimeToSign.com **or call (321) 726-9466**

Sing Along CD **(music CD)**

Learning Spanish has never been so easy and fun! Spanish as a second language will help your young child get a jump start on becoming a lifetime language learner so buy this award-winning bilingual CD today.

We want to help you fight children's obesity with this Physical Fitness CD!

Delight as your child learns Spanish **along with keeping fit with these fun bilingual songs.**

Concepts such as Adding Numbers, Spelling in Spanish, Getting Ready for Your Day, Five Little Monkeys, Position, Weather and Body Parts are introduced in this Boca Beth bilingual music CD for kids of all ages!

Help your child learn more than 200 words and 90 phrases in just this one CD ... all with sing along songs that introduce Spanish and English!

- See more at: http://www.bocabeth.com/bilingual-products-to-teach-spanish-and-english/music-cds/#sthash.0aTupgiJ.dpuf

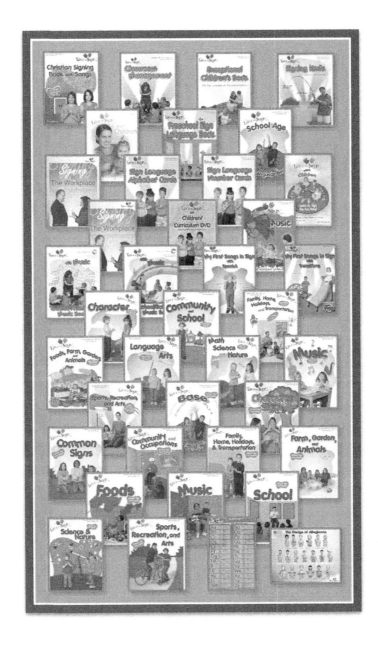

**For additional Time to Sign products please visit our website
www.TimeToSign.com**

Time to Sign with Children DVD

10 topical signing areas, 17 songs, and 3 stories

Our most popular DVD, children learn to sign the fun way with Time to Sign founder Lillian Hubler and friends in this 53-minute video your children will want to watch over and over again!

Topics include the alphabet, numbers, greetings, family, manners, colors, animals, food, and utensils, as well as a section just for parents and teachers, Benefits of Signing with Children.

Songs include the ABCs Song; BINGO; Hands Can Count; Six Little Ducks; Three Little Monkeys; Please & Thank You; Apples & Bananas; Muffin Man; Itsy Bitsy Spider; Row, Row, Row Your Boat; Twinkle, Twinkle Little Star; Where is Thumbkin?; If You're Happy & You Know It; and many more!

Stories include Tea Please; Peek-A-Boo Pets; The Colorful Tiger

Perfect for educators of young children to learn and teach American Sign Language (ASL) in the classroom!

PO Box 33831
Indialantic, FL 32903
Phone 321.259.0976
www.timetosign.com

Contact us at 321.259.0976 or contact@timetosign.com for more information!

...bringing Spanish to life!

Introduce Spanish to Your Children with Award Winning Boca Beth Products

Mi casa/My House DVD

- Learn more than 100 words and 15 phrases in Spanish and English
- Subtitles provide beginning reading practice and parent/provider comfort
- Filmed in 4 six-minute segments with BOCA as the teacher
- Stimulating music and bright images engage the young learner
- 30 minutes, Ages 3 months-6 years

I Like Animals/Me gustan los animales DVD

- Enjoy four song & dance segments showcasing multi-cultural children
- Hear and read more than 200 words and 80 phrases in Spanish and English
- BOCA the puppet joins animals from around the world & neighborhood
- Bonus Boca Beth interactive class featured in this DVD
- 50 minutes, Ages 6 months - 10 years

BOCA The Puppet

- Made in the USA
- Machine wash & dry
- Toy tested - safe for tumble play
- Puppets help bring out the language in your child - native & new

Coloring and Activity Book/ Un libro para colorear y de actividades

- Bilingual - Spanish and English
- Pronunciation guide provided for both languages
- Back to the basics coloring for young children
- Maze, crossword puzzle, matching and comparison fun
- BOCA the language amigo is on almost every page

My First Songs In Spanish/Mis primeras canciones en Inglés Music CD

- Listen & Learn more than 100 words and 40 phrases in Spanish and English
- The basics of counting, days of the week, manner words, greetings, colors, animals and so much more
- Classic children's melodies are the backdrop for our bilingual songs
- Promotes early reading skills when used with Boca Beth free resources
- Ages birth and up

More Boca Beth/Más Boca Beth Music CD

- Enjoy learning more than 150 words & 30 phrases
- Songs about family, seasons, opposites, shapes, telling time and more
- No second language experience required to use this with children
- FREE circle time activities for each song on www.bocabeth.com
- Ages birth and up

Sing Along with Boca Beth /Canta con Boca Beth Music CD

- Fitness CD - Beat children's obesity with these bilingual beats
- FREE suggested fitness activities available online at bocabeth.com
- Learn more than 200 words and 90 phrases on this one music CD
- Sing about weather, five little monkeys, getting ready for your day, and more
- Ages 8 months and up

Musical Shakers: Eggs and Mini-Maracas

- Toy tested, lead free, and durable
- Perfectly sized for children ages 4 months to eight years
- Bright colors - choice of six
- Children love to see BOCA on each shaker

Order online today at bocabeth.com or call toll free 877.825.2622 now!

MICHAEL & LILLIAN HUBLER

ABOUT THE AUTHORS

Michael and Lillian Hubler founded Time to Sign, Inc. in 2000. The company was founded because the Hubler's' recognized the benefits of using American Sign Language (ASL) with their children; and then to other children, families, educators, and care givers around the world. Time to Sign programs have been used in Family Childcares, Private Preschools, Early Head Start, Head Start, and School Districts.

Lillian is a nationally acclaimed presenter/trainer. Since 2000, she has trained over 50,000 educators, parents and children around the world in age appropriate and developmentally appropriate sign language usage. She is renowned for her high energy workshops and presentations. She has appeared on CNN, ABC, NBC, as we'll as interviewed by Florida Today and the Washington Post.

Michael is Director of Educational Curriculum and Product Development for Time to Sign. He is currently working on his doctorate dissertation in the field of education, specializing in the positive impacts of sign language on social and emotional development. Michael has served as an executive director for various educational and community services organizations, specializing in services and programs to enhance the education, personal growth, and development of at-risk children.
Michael and Lillian also owned a licensed day care with 135 children from birth to 12 years of age. They have written over 25 sign language books including preschool and school-age curriculums. Time to Sign's trainings and materials are uniquely designed to promote social emotional development and reduce children's challenging behavior in social settings. Their training programs and materials also promote literacy, language development, and communication.

Made in the USA
Middletown, DE
13 May 2023

30533903R00040